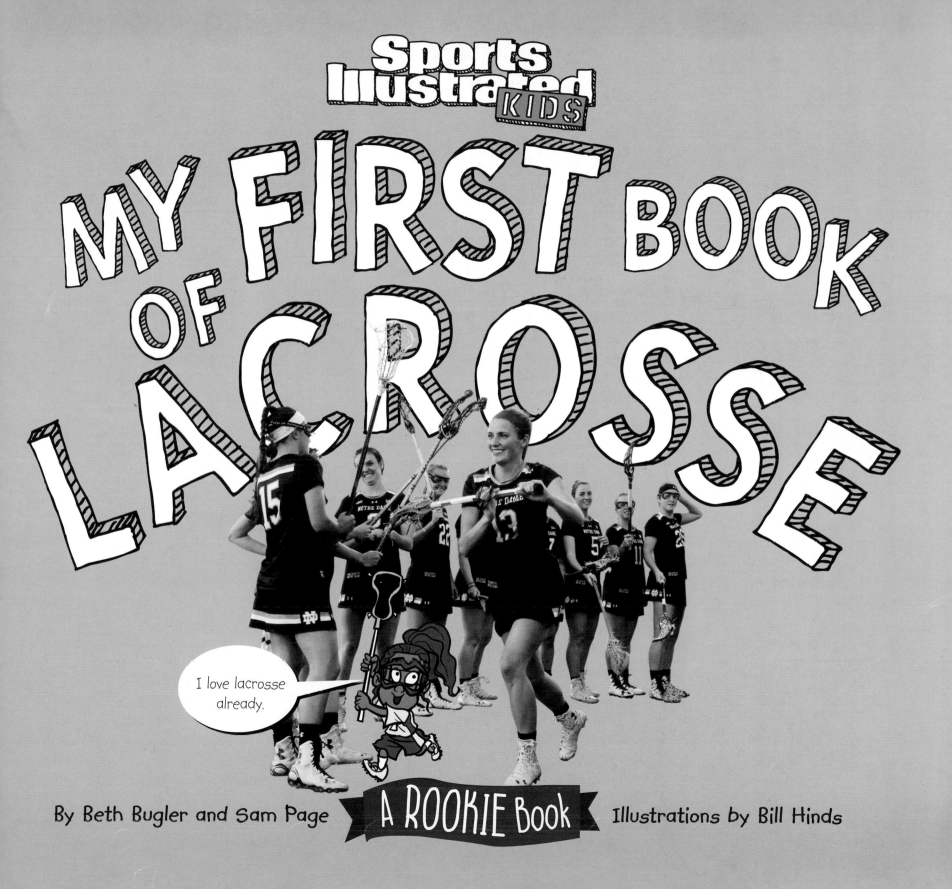

MY FIRST BOOK OF LACROSSE

Sports Illustrated KIDS

I love lacrosse already.

By Beth Bugler and Sam Page

A ROOKIE Book

Illustrations by Bill Hinds

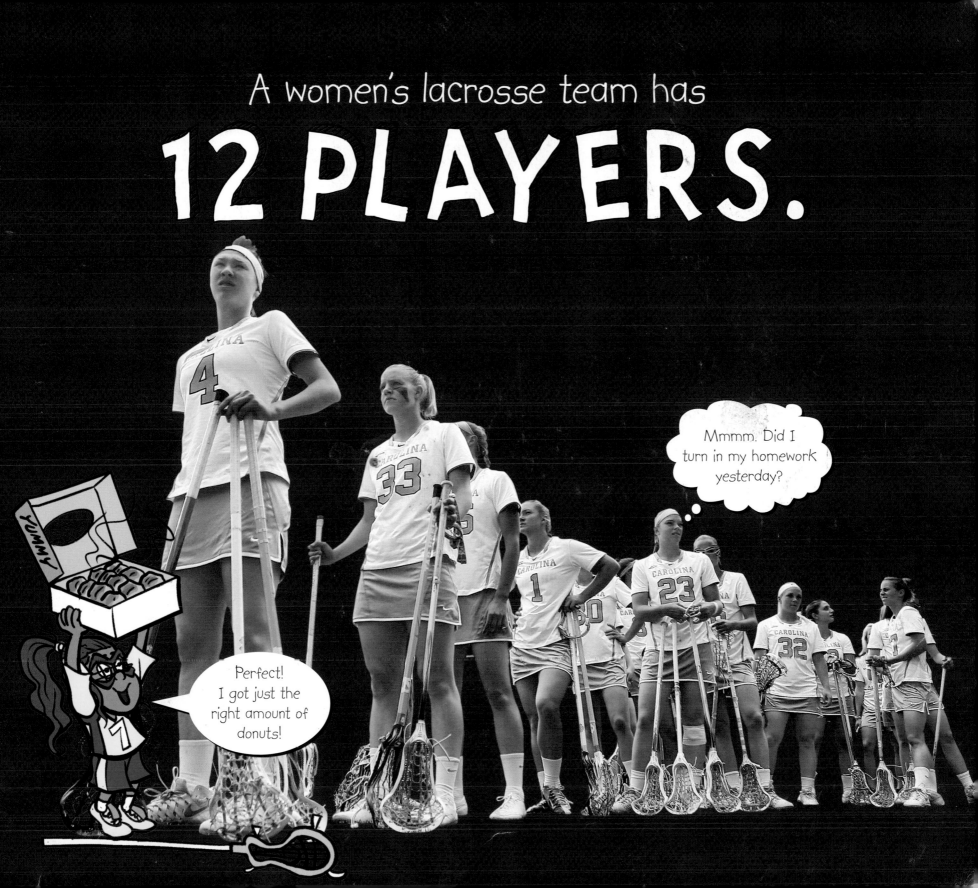

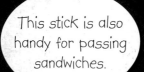

The object of the game is to score goals by using a

STICK

to shoot the ball into a

NET.

This stick is also handy for passing sandwiches.

The rules and equipment used by men and women are different.

MEN

WOMEN

HEAD

HEAD

The **POCKET** of the men's stick is deep to make it easier to hang on to the ball when a player is bumped or poked.

The women's stick has a shallower pocket.

SHAFT
→

SHAFT
←

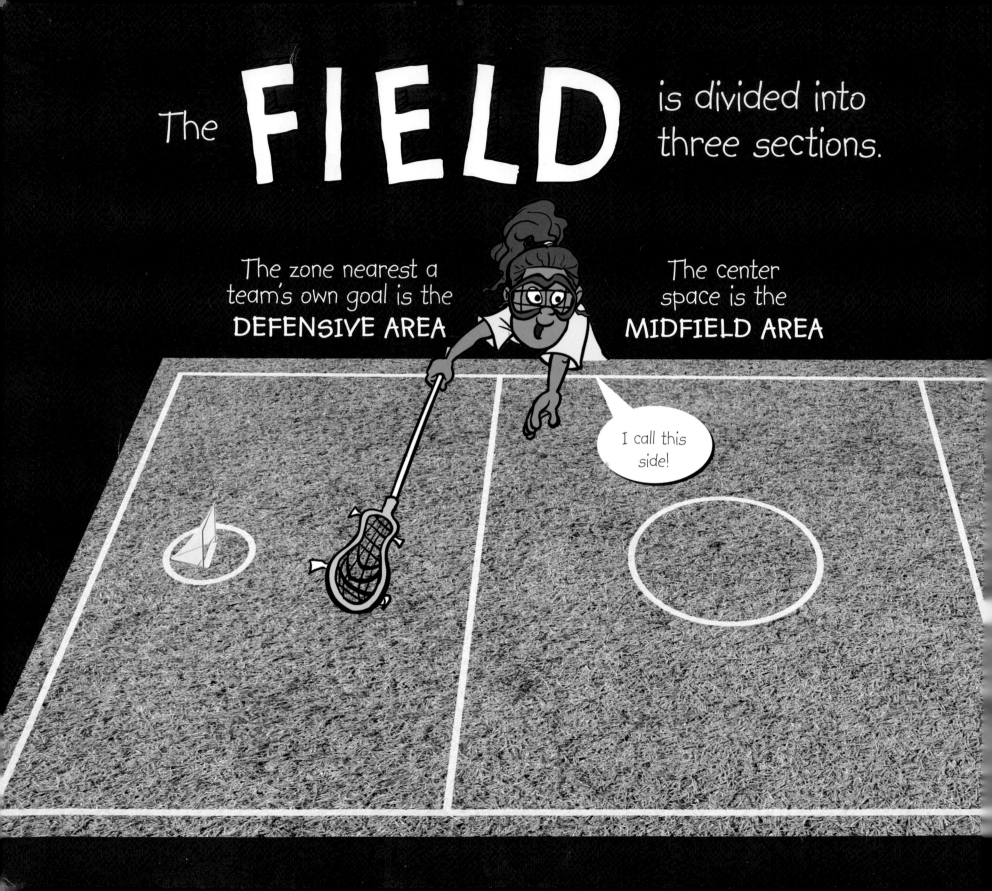

Each goal is surrounded by a circle called the

CREASE.

The section closest to the other team's goal is the **ATTACK AREA**

It doesn't feel like a crease.

The game is usually divided into

FOUR QUARTERS

that are

15 MINUTES each.

The players have different positions and jobs.

ATTACKERS try to score goals.

DEFENDERS stop the attackers from scoring.

MIDFIELDERS help score goals AND try to keep the other team from scoring.

The
GOALIE
uses a stick with a
big head to stop shots from
getting into the net.

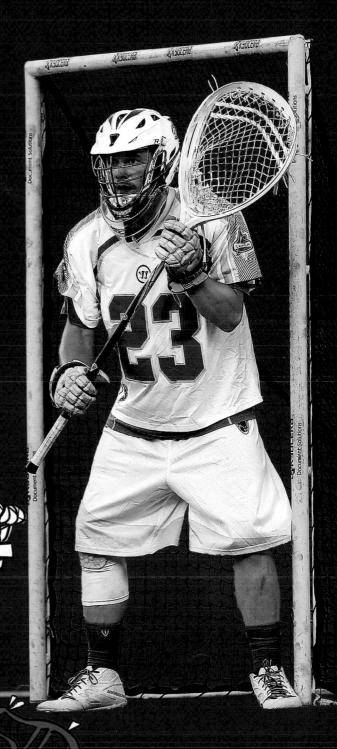

The game begins with a

FACE-OFF.

The ball is placed at the center
of the field, and two midfielders
compete to trap the ball and

SCOOP

it up with their stick.

QUARTER
1ST

The midfielder makes a **PASS** to her

As the player runs with
the ball, he turns his wrist
back and forth to

CRADLE

the ball in the pocket so
it won't fall out.

You're gonna
rock that ball
to sleep.

Clack! The defender knocks the ball away from his opponent with a

STICK CHECK.

QUARTER
2ND

That first quarter went by fast!
Now it's back to the center of the field.
The face-off for women is called the

DRAW.

Oooh! She's got the new Model XII stick!

Oh. So I don't need this?

Does he really expect me to catch that?

The goalie stops the shot. Now he

CLEARS

the ball away from the scoring area by throwing it up the field.

The attacker scoops up the ball and heads toward the goal area.

Did you see that? He turned quickly to

DODGE

the defender. Now he's in position to shoot.

She takes a

SHOT.

Will the ball make it
past the goalie?

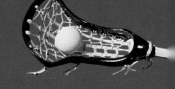

Nope! The shot misses
the goal and the ball goes

OUT OF BOUNDS.

Since an attacking player was
closest to the ball when it crossed
the end line, her team
gets the ball back.

Hi! What's
going on back
here?

That's the end of the half. Time for a *break*!

HALFT

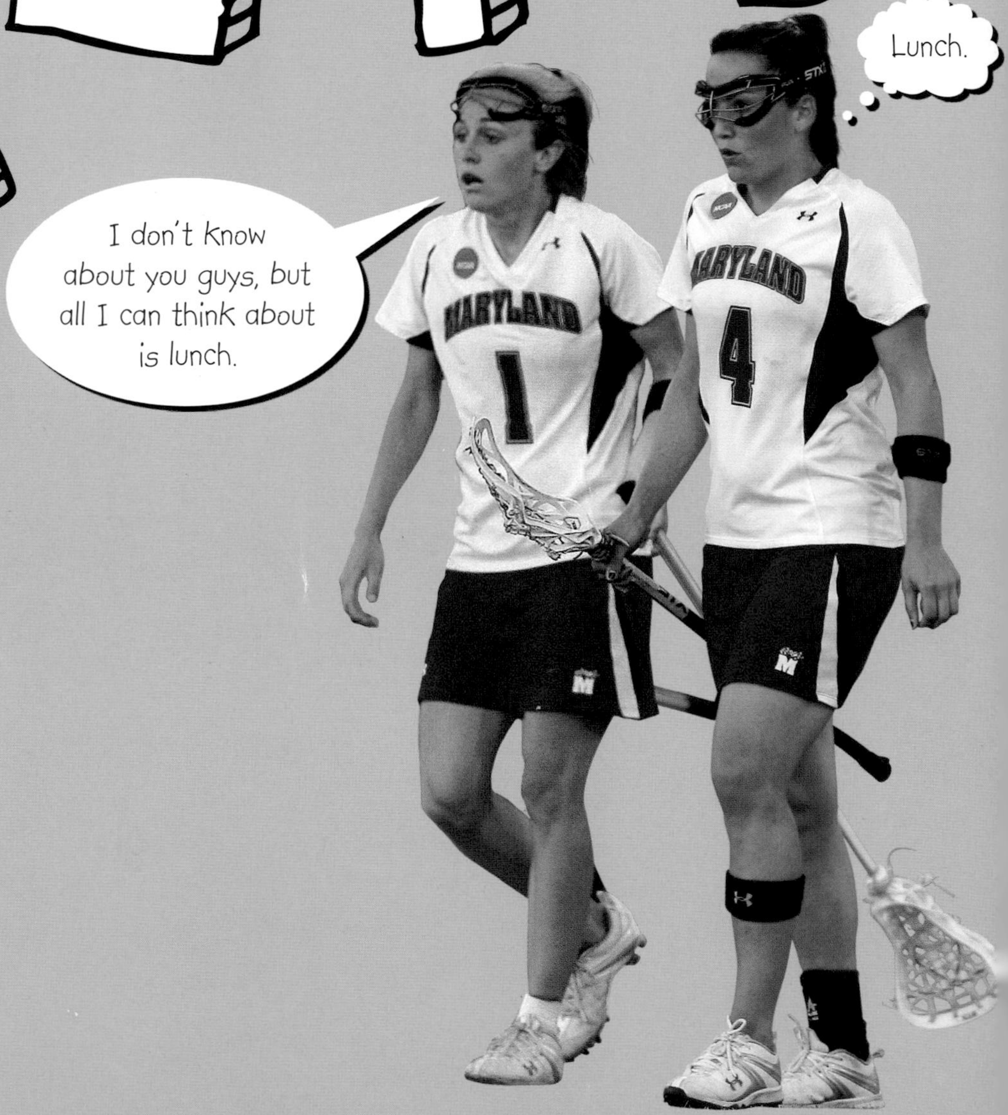

The players fight for the ball in another face-off to start the second half.

No one wins it, and the ball squirts away. It's a

LOOSE BALL.

MINE!

The players all scramble to gain possession.

BNZZZZZZ

QUARTER
3RD

I am Number 1!

I mean . . . SLASHING!

Yowza! A player hit his opponent on the arm, so the referee calls him for

SLASHING.

Now the penalized team must play

MAN DOWN.

They have one fewer player on the field.

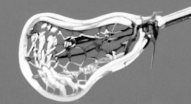

Gonna zig . . .

. . . and zag . . .

The teams battle for the lead. Seeing an opening, the attacker

CUTS

around the defender toward the net.

TIME
1:25

A teammate

FEEDS
her a pass.

She shoots the ball into the net,
but she was inside the crease,
so the goal doesn't count.

That reminds me.
I brought lunch.

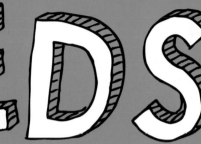

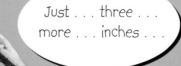

Wait a minute, there are too many players in the attacking area of the field.

That is

OFFSIDES

and a penalty.

I want to help. But I can't!

Their team is behind by one goal. Maybe they should consider a new strategy.

They get together in a

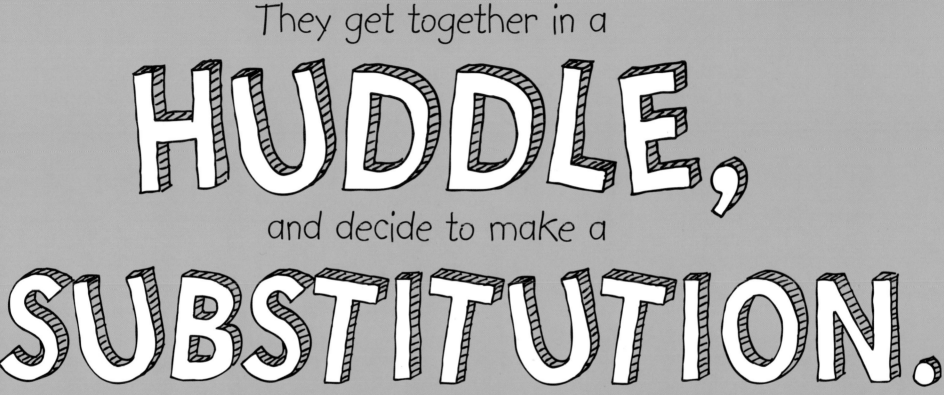

HUDDDLE,

and decide to make a

SUBSTITUTION.

A player will come off the field and
a new one will take her place.

QUARTER **4TH**

Yeah! The new player scored just before the clock ran out! The game is tied!

That means we're going to

SUDDEN DEATH.

Can't look.

Four more minutes will be put on the clock. The first team to score will win.

Writers: Beth Bugler, Sam Page
Designer: Beth Bugler
Illustrator: Bill Hinds
Lacrosse Advisers: Mary Leonard, Bob Page
Production Manager: Hillary Leary

Published by Liberty Street, an imprint of
Time Inc. Books
225 Liberty Street
New York, NY 10281

LIBERTY STREET and SPORTS ILLUSTRATED
KIDS are trademarks of Time Inc. All other
trademarks belong to their respective owners.

ISBN: 978-1-68330-078-6
Library of Congress Control Number: 2017959535

First edition, 2018
1 TLF 18
10 9 8 7 6 5 4 3 2 1

We welcome your comments and suggestions
about Time Inc. Books.

Time Inc. Books
Attention: Book Editors
P.O. Box 62310
Tampa, FL 33662-2310
(800) 765-6400

timeincbooks.com

Time Inc. Books products may be purchased for
business or promotional use. For information on
bulk purchases, please contact Christi Crowley in
the Special Sales Department at (845) 895-9858.

PHOTO CREDITS, in order:
iStockPhoto/Getty Images (cover); Andy Mead/
YCJ/Icon Sportswire/Getty Images (title page);
Rich Barnes/Getty Images (10 players);
Andy Mead/YCJ/Icon Sportswire/AP (12 players);
iStockPhoto/Getty Images (stick, net);
Dustin Bradford/Getty Images (attackers);
Jim Rogash/Getty Images (goalie);
Doug Pensinger/Getty Image (face-off);
Rich Barnes/Getty Images (pass, 2); Jen Fuller/
Getty Images (cradle); Claus Andersen/Getty
Images (stick check); Andy Mead/Icon
Sportswire/Corbis via Getty Images (draw);
Andy Mead/Icon Sportswire/Corbis/Getty
Images (fast break); Jonathan Newton/The
Washington Post/Getty Images (save);
Larry French/NCAA Photos/Getty Images
(dodge, 2); Mitchell Layton/Getty Images (shot);
Matthias Hangst/Bongarts/Getty Images
(out of bounds); Rob Carr/AP (halftime);
Jamie Sabau/Getty Images (loose ball);
Tom Szczerbowski/Getty Images (slashing);
Joel Auerbach/Getty Images (penalty);
Andy Mead/YCJ/Icon Sportswire/Getty Images
(man down); Matthias Hangst/Bongarts/Getty
Images (cuts, feeds); Mitchell Layton/Getty
Images (offsides); Andy Mead/YCJ/Icon
Sportswire/Getty Images (huddle);
John McDonnell/The Washington Post/Getty
Images (sudden death, score); Omar Rawlings/
Getty Images (game over, 2); Rich Barnes/Getty
Images (back cover)